500

REALLY USEFUL

FRENCH
WORDS
AND PHRASES

Written and edited by
Carol Watson and Philippa Moyle

Illustrated by
Teresa Foster

Contents

Watts

LONDON • NEW YORK • SYDNEY

This book was created by Times Four Publishing Ltd, 5 High Street, Cuckfield, Sussex RH17 5EN

The consultant, Katherine Folliot, was born and brought up in France. She has an MA in Modern Languages from the Sorbonne in Paris. She now teaches French in England.

Pronunciation guide: Philippa Tomlinson, Kay Barnham

Editor: Philippa Moyle
Senior Editor: Nicola Wright
Designers: Jane Felstead, Suzie Hooper, Jenny Searle, Jonathan Skelton
Design Manager: Kate Buxton
Series concept: Tony Potter

Colour separations by RCS Graphics Ltd, Leeds
Printed by Proost, Belgium

First published in 1993 by Watts Books

Copyright © 1993 Times Four Publishing Ltd

BRITISH LIBRARY CATALOGUING IN PUBLICATION DATA
A catalogue record for this book is available from the British Library.

Dewey Decimal Classification: 448.1

UK ISBN 0 7496 1182 0

10 9 8 7 6 5 4 3 2 1

About this book

In this book you will find out how to speak French. You will meet the Flaubert family who will show you what to say in many different situations. Here they are to introduce themselves.

Nous nous appelons Monsieur et Madame Flaubert.
(Noo noo zapperlong Mersyer ay Madam Flowbair.)
We are Monsieur and Madame Flaubert.

Je m'appelle Marie.
(Jer mappell Marie.)
My name is Marie.

Je m'appelle Jean.
(Jer mappell Jong.)
My name is Jean.

Everything the Flaubert family says is written in French and English. There is also a guide to pronouncing the French words.

these are the French words

Je m'appelle Marie.

this shows you how to pronounce the French

(Jer mappell Marie.)

My name is Marie.

this is what it means in English

How to speak French

The pronunciation guide shows you how to say the French words. These notes will help you to use the guide:

- When you see the letters 'ew', purse your lips as if you are going to make an 'oo' sound, but say 'ee' instead.
- The letters 'er' are pronounced like the 'er' in under.

- You should say the letters 'ng' very quickly, so that the 'g' is almost silent. It should sound like the 'ng' of the word 'bang'.
- The letter 'į' is pronounced like the 's' in 'treasure'.

Accents

- French vowels often have marks called accents above them, such as **é**, **à** or **î**. Vowels with accents are pronounced differently from vowels without accents.

- The letter 'c' sometimes has an accent underneath it, eg in the word '**ç**a'. This letter 'c' should be pronounced like the 's' in 'sock', not like the 'c' in 'cat'.

Speaking to people

In French, there are two different words for 'you'. You use **tu** when you speak to a friend or an adult you know well. You use **vous** when you speak to more than one friend or an adult you do not know very well.

Masculine and feminine words

In French, some words are masculine and some are feminine. There are different words for 'the':

le salon   (masculine singular)
la porte   (feminine singular)

When the word begins with a vowel you use **l'**, eg **l'**église.

All plural words have the same word for 'the':

les salons (masculine plural)
les portes (feminine plural)

Meeting people

French people have different ways of greeting someone they meet. They use very polite greetings for people they do not know well and more friendly greetings for close friends.

Monsieur Flaubert meets a man he does not know very well.

> **Bonjour!**
> *(Bongjoor!)*
> Good morning!

> **Comment allez-vous?**
> *(Commong tallay-voo?)*
> How are you?

> **Bonjour, Monsieur Flaubert.**
> *(Bongjoor, Mersyer Flowbair.)*
> Good morning, Mr Flaubert.

> **Très bien, merci.**
> *(Tray beeyang, mairsee.)*
> Very well, thank you.

Marie and Jean meet their friends outside the shops.

> **Salut, ça va?**
> *(Salew, sah vah?)*
> Hello, how're you doing?

> **Ça va merci, et toi?**
> *(Sah vah mairsee, ay twah?)*
> Fine thank you, and you?

> **A bientôt.**
> *(Ah beeyangtoh.)*
> See you soon.

> **Au revoir.**
> *(Orvwahr.)*
> Goodbye.

Monsieur Flaubert welcomes visitors to his home for dinner.

Bonsoir!
(Bongswahr!)
Good evening!

The phrase 'Bonne nuit' is only used last thing at night.

Bonne nuit, maman.
(Bonn nwee, mamong.)
Good night, Mummy.

Bonne nuit, Jean.
(Bonn nwee, Jong.)
Good night, Jean.

When people meet, they often like to discuss the weather. You will find some phrases describing the weather on page 31.

'Bonjour' can also mean 'good afternoon' as well as 'good morning'.

BOUCHERIE

Bonjour, Madame. Il fait beau aujourd'hui, n'est-ce pas?
(Bongjoor, Madam. Eel fay boh ohjoordwee, nesspah?)
Good afternoon, madam. It's a fine day, isn't it?

Oui, il fait chaud.
(Wee, eel fay shoh.)
Yes, it is hot.

5

Making friends

The Flaubert family is at the beach for the day.
Monsieur and Madame Flaubert are sunbathing with
the rest of the family while Marie and Jean are
busy making friends.

Bonjour, comment tu t'appelles?
(Bongjoor, commong tew tappell?)
Hello, what is your name?

Je m'appelle Edward, et toi?
(Jer mappell Edward, ay twah?)
My name is Edward, and yours?

Je m'appelle Marie. Quel âge as-tu?
(Jer mappell Marree. Kell ahj ah-tew?)
My name is Marie. How old are you?

J'ai dix ans.
(Jay deez ong.)
I am ten.

Tu habites où?
(Tew abbeet oo?)
Where do you live?

J'habite en Angleterre.
(Jabbeett onong-glertair.)
I live in England.

Marie and Edward introduce their brother and sister.

Voici mon frère Jean.
(Vwahsee mong frair Jong.)
This is my brother Jean.

Voici ma soeur Emily.
(Vwahsee mah serr Emily.)
This is my sister Emily.

Tu parles français?
(Tew pahrl frongssay?)
Do you speak French?

Pardon, je ne comprends pas.
(Pahrdong, jer ner comprong pah.)
Sorry, I do not understand.

The other members of the Flaubert family enjoy a restful afternoon.

la famille
(lah fammeeyer)
family

le père
(ler pair)
father

la grand-mère
(lah grong-mair)
grandmother

la mère
(lah mair)
mother

l'oncle
(longkler)
uncle

la tante
(lah tongt)
aunt

le grand-père
(ler grong-pair)
grandfather

7

Finding the way

Madame Flaubert and her children visit a town that they have not been to before.

Pardon Madame, y a t'il un café près d'ici?
(Pahrdong Madam, eeyateel ung kaffay pray deessee?)
Excuse me, is there a café near here?

Oui, Madame.
(Wee, Madam.)
Yes, madam.

C'est loin?
(Say lwang?)
Is it far?

Merci.
(Mairsee.)
Thank you.

C'est au coin de la rue.
(Say toh kwang der lah rew.)
It is on the corner of the street.

Je vous en prie.
(Jer voo zong pree.)
It is a pleasure.

Direction words

à gauche *(ah gohsh)* left	**derrière** *(derryair)* behind	**devant** *(dervong)* in front of	**à droite** *(ah drwaht)* right
à côté de *(ah kohtay der)* next to	**tout droit** *(too drwah)* straight on		**en face de** *(ong fass der)* opposite
jusqu'à *(jewsskah)* as far as	**près d'ici** *(pray deessee)* near here	**là-bas** *(lah-bah)* over there	**entre** *(ongtrer)* between

On their way to the station, Marie and Jean get lost.

Places to ask for

la gendarmerie
(lah jongdarmeree)
police station

la cabine téléphonique
(lah kabbeen taylayfoneek)
telephone box

l'église
(laygleez)
church

l'hôpital
(lohpeetahl)
hospital

les toilettes
(lay twahlett)
toilets

Staying in a hotel or house

Monsieur and Madame Flaubert are on holiday at a hotel. While they are away, Marie and Jean stay at their grandparents' house.

Je voudrais réserver une chambre.
(Jer voodray rayzairvay ewn shongbrer.)
I would like to book a room.

Oui, Monsieur. Que désirez-vous?
(Wee, Mersyer. Ker dayzeeray-voo?)
Yes, sir. What would you like?

Une chambre pour deux personnes.
(Ewn shongbrer poor der pairsonn.)
A double room.

Le dîner est à quelle heure?
(Ler deenay ay tah kell err?)
What time is dinner?

A huit heures, Madame.
(Ah weet err, Madam.)
At eight o'clock, madam.

Voici votre clef, Monsieur.
(Vwahsee vottrer klay, Mersyer.)
Here is your key, sir.

le porteur
(ler porterr)
porter

la valise
(lah valeez)
suitcase

l'ascenseur
(lassongserr)
lift

la clef
(lah klay)
key

le toit
(ler twah)
roof

la maison
(lah mayzong)
house

le grenier
(ler grernyay)
attic

la salle de bains
(lah sall der bang)
bathroom

la fenêtre
(lah fernettrer)
window

la chambre
(lah shongbrer)
bedroom

le lit
(ler lee)
bed

la douche
(lah doosh)
shower

le sol
(ler soll)
floor

l'armoire
(larmwahr)
wardrobe

le fauteuil
(ler fohter-yer)
armchair

le salon
(ler sallong)
living room

la porte
(lah port)
door

la télévision
(lah taylayveezyong)
television

la cuisine
(lah kweezeen)
kitchen

la salle à manger
(lah sallamongjay)
dining room

la chaise
(lah shehz)
chair

la table
(lah tahbler)
table

l'escalier
(leskalyay)
staircase

Camping

le matelas pneumatique
(ler matterlah pnermatteek)
lilo

le lit de camp
(ler lee der cong)
camp bed

l'eau
(loh)
water

le piquet
(ler peekay)
tent peg

Eau Potable

(Oh pohtahbler)
Drinking water

le réchaud
(ler rayshoh)
stove

It is the summer holidays. The Flaubert family is staying at a campsite that provides its own tents which are very comfortable.

Où est-ce que je peux prendre une douche?
(Oo essker jer per prongdrer ewn doosh?)
Where can I take a shower?

Là-bas, je crois.
(Lah-bah, jer crwah.)
Over there, I think.

(Rayzairvay oh caravan)
Caravans only

Réservé aux Caravanes

le tapis de sol
(ler tappee der soll)
groundsheet

la tente
(lah tongt)
tent

la caravane
(lah caravan)
caravan

le maillet
(ler my-yay)
mallet

Je vais au magasin du camping.
(Jer vay zoh magazang dew congpeeng.)
I am going to the campsite shop.

Attends-moi!
(Attong-mwah!)
Wait for me!

le terrain de camping
(ler tairang der congpeeng)
campsite

TOILETTES
(Twahlett)
Toilets

la remorque
(lah rermork)
trailer

parking Interdit
(Parkeeng angtairdee)
No parking

le camping gaz
(ler congpeeng gaz)
camping gas

le sac de couchage
(ler sack der cooshahj)
sleeping bag

Going shopping

The Flaubert family is out shopping. They visit the baker, the market and the newsagent.

The baker

> **Bonjour. Je voudrais deux pains, s'il vous plaît.**
> *(Bongjoor. Jer voodray der pang, seelvooplay.)*
> Hello. I would like two loaves of bread, please.

> **Oui, bien sûr. C'est tout?**
> *(Wee, beeyang sewr. Say too?)*
> Yes, certainly. Is that all?

> **Ça fait combien?**
> *(Sah fay combeeyang?)*
> How much is that?

> **Ça fait sept francs cinquante, Madame.**
> *(Sah fay sett frong sangkongt, Madam.)*
> That is seven francs fifty centimes, madam.

French money is divided into francs (F) and centimes (ct). There are 100 centimes in one franc. The numbers you will need to know for shopping are on page 31.

The market

> **Madame, vous désirez?**
> *(Madam, voo dayzeeray?)*
> Can I help you, madam?

> **Un kilo de tomates, s'il vous plaît.**
> *(Ung keeloh der tommaht, seelvooplay.)*
> A kilo of tomatoes, please.

les pommes
(lay pomm)
apples

les tomates
(lay tommaht)
tomatoes

The newsagent

Combien coûtent les cartes postales?
(Combeeyang coot lay cart postahl?)
How much are the postcards?

Je voudrais un journal, s'il vous plaît.
(Jer voodray ung joornahl, seelvooplay.)
I would like a newspaper, please.

Ça fait trois francs, Monsieur.
(Sah fay trwah frong, Mersyer.)
That is three francs, sir.

Deux francs la carte.
(Der frong lah cart.)
Two francs each.

Shopping words

faire des courses
(fair day coorss)
to go shopping

je voudrais
(jer voodray)
I would like

je regarde seulement
(jer rergard serlermong)
I am only looking

acheter
(ashtay)
to buy

coûter
(cootay)
to cost

un kilo
(ung keeloh)
a kilo

un litre
(ung leetrer)
a litre

ouvert
(oovair)
open

soldes
(solld)
sale

une livre
(ewn leevrer)
half a kilo

Combien coûte...?
(Combeeyang coot...?)
How much is...?

libre service
(leebrer sairveess)
self-service

les poires
(lay pwahr)
pears

les pommes de terre
(lay pomm der tair)
potatoes

les carottes
(lay carott)
carrots

les choux
(lay shoo)
cabbages

15

The post office and bank

Marie and Edward visit the post office while Madame Flaubert is at the bank.

Combien coûte un timbre pour une carte postale pour l'Angleterre?
(Combeeyang coot ung tangbrer poor ewn cart postahl poor long-glertair?)
How much is a stamp for a postcard to England?

Deux francs.
(Der frong.)
Two francs.

Je voudrais quatre timbres, s'il vous plaît.
(Jer voodray kahtrer tangbrer, seelvooplay.)
I would like four stamps, please.

Oui, bien sûr.
(Wee, beeyang sewr.)
Yes, certainly.

Où se trouve la boîte aux lettres?
(Oo ser troov lah bwaht oh lettrer?)
Where is the post box?

Là-bas.
(Lah-bah.)
Over there.

POSTES

la lettre
(lah lettrer)
letter

le timbre
(ler tangbrer)
stamp

la télécopie
(lah taylaycoppee)
fax

la télécarte
(lah taylaycart)
telephone card

Pourriez-vous me donner de la monnaie?
(Pooreeay-voo mer donnay der lah monnay?)
Could I have some small change?

Puis-je changer un chèque de voyage ici?
(Pwee-jer shongjay ung sheck der vwah-yahj eessee?)
Can I cash a traveller's cheque here?

le billet
(ler beeyay)
bank note

la pièce
(lah pyess)
coin

le chèque de voyage
(ler sheck der vwah-yahj)
traveller's cheque

la monnaie
(lah monnay)
small change

17

Eating out

French people enjoy going out with friends and family for a drink or a meal.

Madame Flaubert meets a friend at a café.

Deux cafés, s'il vous plaît.
(Der kaffay, seelvooplay.)
Two coffees, please.

Bien sûr, Madame.
(Beeyang sewr, Madam.)
Certainly, madam.

The Flaubert family visits the countryside and enjoys a picnic in the sunshine.

Je voudrais une tranche de quiche.
(Jer voodray ewn trangsh der keesh.)
I would like a slice of quiche.

Sers-toi.
(Sair-twah.)
Help yourself.

le pique-nique
(ler peek-neek)
picnic

J'ai faim.
(Jay fang.)
I am hungry.

Veux-tu un sandwich au jambon?
(Ver-too ung songdweech oh jangbong?)
Would you like a ham sandwich?

It is Madame Flaubert's birthday. She and Monsieur Flaubert dine at a restaurant.

Useful words for eating out

Madame *(Madam)* waitress				**Monsieur** *(Mersyer)* waiter
	le menu *(ler mernew)* menu	**la serviette** *(lah sairveeyett)* napkin	**l'addition** *(laddeessyong)* bill	
la nappe *(lah napp)* tablecloth	**le couteau** *(ler kootoh)* knife	**la fourchette** *(lah foorshett)* fork	**la cuillère** *(lah kweeyair)* spoon	**le verre** *(ler vair)* glass

Visiting places

Monsieur and Madame Flaubert like to take their children to the cinema and other places of entertainment.

Madame Flaubert takes Jean and Pierre to see a cartoon film.

The Flaubert family often visits the tourist information centre.
It has leaflets that show interesting places to visit.

le centre de loisir
(ler songtrer der lwahzeer)
leisure centre

les grottes
(lay grott)
caves

le théâtre
(ler tayahtrer)
theatre

le château
(ler shattoh)
castle

The Flaubert family visits a sound and light show at a château. The show is called a 'son et lumière' *(sonnay lewmeeair)*. It tells the history of the château.

C'est très joli.
(Say tray jollee.)
It is very pretty.

Je suis fatigué.
(Jer swee fateegay.)
I am tired.

C'est intéressant, n'est-ce pas?
(Say tangtairessang, nesspah?)
It is interesting, isn't it?

le cirque
(ler seerk)
circus

la réserve nationale
(lah raysairv nassyonal)
nature reserve

le musée
(ler mewzay)
museum

Games and sports

le rugby
(ler rergbee)
rugby

le golf
(ler golf)
golf

le football
(ler footbohll)
football

le ski
(ler skee)
skiing

la planche à voile
(lah plongsh ah vwahl)
windsurfing

l'aviron
(laveerong)
rowing

le ski nautique
(ler skee nohteek)
water skiing

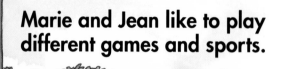

Marie and Jean like to play different games and sports.

la balançoire
(lah ballongswahr)
swing

C'est à toi.
(Say tah twah.)
Your turn.

Est-ce que je peux jouer?
(Essker jer per jooay?)
Can I play?

les billes
(lay beeyer)
marbles

l'équitation
(laykitassyong)
riding

le patinage
(ler patteenahj)
skating

faire du jogging
(fair dew jogging)
to go jogging

le badminton
(ler badmeengtong)
badminton

la natation
(lah nahtassyong)
swimming

Attrape!
(Attrapp!)
Catch!

cache-cache
(cash-cash)
hide and seek

...Quatre, cinq, six...
(...Kahtrer, sangk, seess...)
...Four, five, six...

la pêche
(lah pesh)
fishing

le tennis
(ler tenneess)
tennis

les boules
(lay booll)
bowls

la gymnastique
(lah jimnasteek)
gymnastics

le volleyball
(ler volleebohll)
volleyball

le cyclisme
(ler seekleezm)
cycling

Accidents and illnesses

In France, there are different telephone numbers for the police, the fire brigade and the ambulance service.

On m'a volé mon sac à main!
(Ong mah vollay mong sak ah mang!)
My handbag has been stolen.

Au feu!
(Oh fer!)
Fire!

Au secours!
(Oh sercoor!)
Help!

Venez vite!
(Vernay veet!)
Come quickly!

Accident words

l'agent de police
(lahjong der pohleess)
policeman

le pompier
(ler pongpyay)
fireman

l'ambulancier
(longbewlongssyay)
ambulance man

la voiture de police
(lah vwahtewr der pohleess)
police car

la voiture de pompiers
(lah vwahtewr der pongpyay)
fire engine

l'ambulance
(longbewlongss)
ambulance

Je me suis fait piquer par une guêpe.
(Jer mer swee fay peekay parr ewn gep.)
I have been stung by a wasp.

J'ai attrapé un coup de soleil.
(Jay attrappay ung coo der sohlay.)
I am sunburnt.

l'aspirine
(laspeereen)
aspirin

le médecin
(ler medsang)
doctor

l'infirmière
(langfermeeair)
nurse

le pansement
(ler pongsmong)
sticking plaster

J'ai mal à la tête.
(Jay mal ah lah tett.)
I have a headache.

Tu as de la fièvre.
(Tew ah der lah feeyairvrer.)
You have a temperature.

Je suis enrhumée.
(Jer swee zongrewmay.)
I have a cold.

J'ai mal au ventre.
(Jay mal oh vongtrer.)
I have a stomach ache.

Travelling

The Flaubert family travels by different kinds of transport.

Nous sommes en panne.
(Noo somm zong pann.)
We have broken down.

Où est le garage le plus proche?
(Oo ay ler garahj ler ploo prosh?)
Where is the nearest garage?

la voiture
(lah vwahtewr)
car

Un billet pour Paris.
(Ung beeyay poor Parree.)
A ticket to Paris.

Railway words

la gare	**la guarde**	**l'horaire**
(lah garr)	*(lah gard)*	*(lorrair)*
station	guard	timetable

le quai	**le guichet**
(ler kay)	*(ler geeshay)*
platform	ticket office

le composteur	**le bagage**	**le billet**
(ler congposterr)	*(ler bagahj)*	*(ler beeyay)*
ticket puncher	luggage	ticket

la voiture-buffet	**le chariot à bagages**
(lah vwahtewr-bewfay)	*(ler sharreeoh ah bagahj)*
buffet car	trolley

L'autobus est en retard.
(Lohtohbooss ay tong retarr.)
The bus is late.

l'autobus
(lohtohbooss)
bus

Jusqu'où allons-nous?
(Jewskoo allong-noo?)
How far are we going?

la bicyclette
(lah beesseeclett)
bicycle

le porteur
(ler porterr)
porter

A quelle heure part le train?
(Ah kel err parr ler trang?)
What time does the train leave?

le train
(ler trang)
train

Bon voyage!
(Bong voyahj!)
Have a good journey!

Au revoir, papa.
(Orvwahr, papah.)
Goodbye, Daddy.

27

More useful words

Time

Quelle heure est-il, s'il te plaît?
(Kell err ayteel, seelterplay?)
What time is it?

Il est trois heures.
(Eel ay trwah zerr.)
It is three o'clock.

Il est trois heures dix.
(Eel ay trwah zerr deess.)
It is ten past three.

Il est trois heures et quart.
(Eel ay trwah zerr ay kahr.)
It is quarter past three.

Il est trois heures et demie.
(Eel ay trwah zerr ay dermee.)
It is half past three.

Il est quatre heures moins le quart.
(Eel ay kahtrer err mwang ler kahr.)
It is quarter to four.

Il est quatre heures moins dix.
(Eel ay kahtrer err mwang deess.)
It is ten minutes to four.

Il est midi.
(Eel ay meedee.)
It is midday.

Il est minuit.
(Eel ay meenwee.)
It is midnight.

Times of the day

l'après-midi
(lappray-meedee)
afternoon

la nuit
(lah nwee)
night

le matin
(ler mattang)
morning

le soir
(ler swahr)
evening

The months of the year and days of the week

janvier
(jongveeay)
January

The French do not use capital letters at the beginning of words for months of the year or days of the week.

juillet
(jweeay)
July

février
(fayvreeay)
February

lundi *(lerngdee)* Monday	**mardi** *(mahrdee)* Tuesday	**mercredi** *(maircrerdee)* Wednesday
	jeudi *(jerdee)* Thursday	**vendredi** *(vongdrerdee)* Friday
samedi *(sammdee)* Saturday		**dimanche** *(deemongsh)* Sunday

août
(oott)
August

mars
(mahrss)
March

septembre
(sayptongbrer)
September

The seasons

le printemps
(ler prangtong)
spring

l'été
(laytay)
summer

octobre
(oktohbrer)
October

avril
(avreel)
April

novembre
(nohvongbrer)
November

mai
(may)
May

l'automne
(lohton)
autumn

l'hiver
(leevair)
winter

décembre
(dayssongbrer)
December

juin
(jwang)
June

Clothes and parts of the body

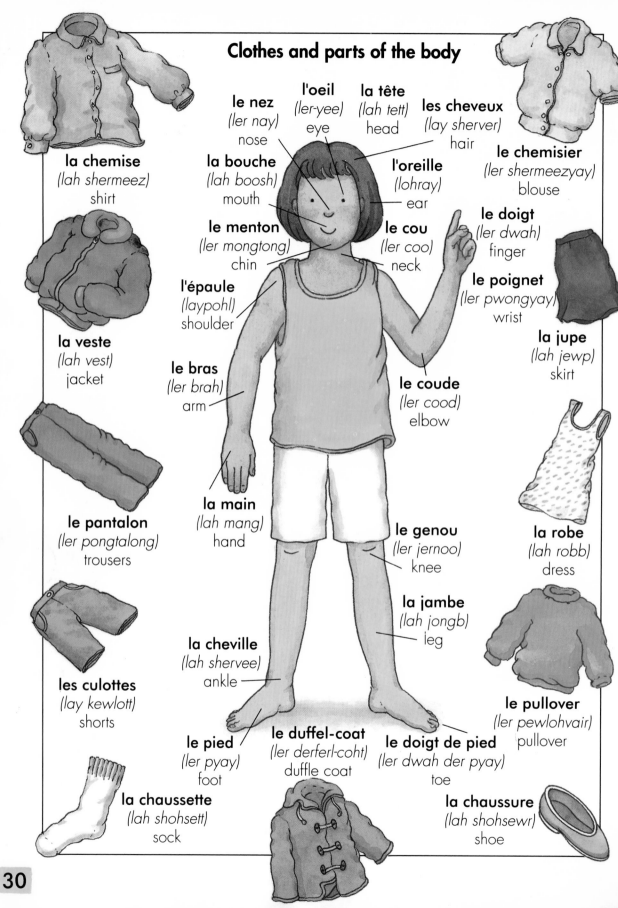

la chemise
(lah shermeez)
shirt

la veste
(lah vest)
jacket

le pantalon
(ler pongtalong)
trousers

les culottes
(lay kewlott)
shorts

le nez
(ler nay)
nose

l'oeil
(ler-yee)
eye

la tête
(lah tett)
head

les cheveux
(lay sherver)
hair

la bouche
(lah boosh)
mouth

l'oreille
(lohray)
ear

le chemisier
(ler shermeezyay)
blouse

le menton
(ler mongtong)
chin

le cou
(ler coo)
neck

le doigt
(ler dwah)
finger

l'épaule
(laypohl)
shoulder

le poignet
(ler pwongyay)
wrist

la jupe
(lah jewp)
skirt

le bras
(ler brah)
arm

le coude
(ler cood)
elbow

la main
(lah mang)
hand

le genou
(ler jernoo)
knee

la robe
(lah robb)
dress

la cheville
(lah shervee)
ankle

la jambe
(lah jongb)
leg

le pied
(ler pyay)
foot

le duffel-coat
(ler derferl-coht)
duffle coat

le doigt de pied
(ler dwah der pyay)
toe

le pullover
(ler pewlohvair)
pullover

la chaussette
(lah shohsett)
sock

la chaussure
(lah shohsewr)
shoe

Colours and numbers

jaune
(johne)
yellow

orange
(oronj)
orange

rouge
(rooj)
red

vert
(vair)
green

1 **un**
(ung)

2 **deux**
(der)

trois **3**
(trwah)

4 **quatre**
(kahtrer) **5**

cinq
(sangk)

6 **six**
(seess)

7 **sept**
(sett)

8 **huit**
(weet)

9 **neuf**
(nerf) **10**

dix
(deess)

11 **onze**
(ongz) **12**

douze
(dooz)

13 **treize**
(trayz) **14**

quatorze
(kattorz)

15 **quinze**
(kangz)

seize
(sayz) **16**

17 **dix-sept**
(dee-sett) **18**

dix-huit
(dee-zweet)

19 **dix-neuf**
(dee-znerf)

blanc
(blong)
white

noir
(nwahr)
black

rose
(roze)
pink

gris
(gree)
grey

The weather

Il fait beau.
(Eel fay boh.)
It is fine.

Il fait froid.
(Eel fay frwah.)
It is cold.

Il fait du soleil.
(Eel fay dew sohlay.)
It is sunny.

Il pleut.
(Eel pler.)
It is raining.

Il fait chaud.
(Eel fay shoh.)
It is hot.

Il fait du vent.
(Eel fay dew vong.)
It is windy.

---

vingt
(vang) **20**

21 **vingt et un**
(vang tay ung)

vingt-deux
(vang-der) **22**

30 **trente**
(trongt)

quarante
(karrongt) **40**

cinquante
(sangkongt) **60**

soixante-dix
(swassongt-deess) **80**

quatre-vingt-dix
(kahtrer-vang-deess)

50 **soixante**
(swassongt) **70**

quatre-vingts
(kahtrer-vang) **90**

bleu
(bler)
blue

cent
(song)
100

mille
(meel)
1,000

million
(meelyong)
1,000,000

brun
(brerng)
brown

Animals

le crocodile
(ler crocohdeel)
crocodile

la baleine
(lah bahlenn)
whale

The verb meaning 'to be' is **être**.

je suis	**nous sommes**
(jer swee)	*(noo somm)*
I am	we are
tu es	**vous êtes**
(tew ay)	*(voo zett)*
you are	you are
il est	**ils sont**
(eel ay)	*(eel song)*
he is	they are (masculine)
elle est	**elles sont**
(ell ay)	*(ell song)*
she is	they are (feminine)

l'ours
(loorss)
bear

le loup
(ler loo)
wolf

le dauphin
(ler dohfang)
dolphin

le panda
(ler pongda)
panda

The verb meaning 'to have' is **avoir**.

j'ai	**nous avons**
(jay)	*(noo zavong)*
I have	we have
tu as	**vous avez**
(tew ah)	*(voo zavay)*
you have	you have
il a	**ils ont**
(eel ah)	*(eel zong)*
he has	they have (masculine)
elle a	**elles ont**
(ell ah)	*(ell zong)*
she has	they have (feminine)

le zèbre
(ler zebrer)
zebra

le tigre
(ler teegrer)
tiger

le gorille
(ler goreeyer)
gorilla

le lion
(ler leeong)
lion

le kangourou
(ler kongooroo)
kangaroo

l'éléphant
(laylayfong)
elephant

la girafe
(lah jeeraff)
giraffe